SCIENTOLOGY
Improving Life in a Troubled World

Founded and developed by L. Ron Hubbard, Scientology is an applied religious philosophy which offers an exact route through which anyone can regain the truth and simplicity of his spiritual self.

Scientology consists of specific axioms that define the underlying causes and principles of existence and a vast area of observations in the humanities, a philosophic body that literally applies to the entirety of life.

This broad body of knowledge resulted in two applications of the subject: first, a technology for man to increase his spiritual awareness and attain the freedom sought by many great philosophic teachings; and, second, a great number of fundamental principles men can use to improve their lives. In fact, in this second application, Scientology offers nothing less than practical methods to better *every* aspect of our existence—means to create new ways of life. And from this comes the subject matter you are about to read.

Compiled from the writings of L. Ron Hubbard, the data presented here is but one of the tools which can be found in *The Scientology Handbook*. A comprehensive guide, the handbook contains numerous applications of Scientology which can be used to improve many other areas of life.

In this booklet, the editors have augmented the data with a short introduction, practical exercises and examples of successful application.

Courses to increase your understanding and further materials to broaden your knowledge are available at your nearest Scientology church, listed at the back of this booklet.

Many new phenomena about man and life are described in Scientology, and so you may encounter terms in these pages you are not familiar with. These are described the first time they appear and in the glossary at the back of the booklet.

Scientology is for use. It is a practical philosophy, something one *does*. Using this data, you *can* change conditions.

Millions of people who want to do something about the conditions they see around them have applied this knowledge. They know that life can be improved. And they know that Scientology works.

Use what you read in these pages to help yourself and others and you will too.

CHURCH OF SCIENTOLOGY INTERNATIONAL

How often have you heard someone say, "I don't understand him"? Sometimes irrational, unforeseen acts seem to be the norm among our fellows.

The fact is, there has never been a workable method to invariably predict human behavior—until now.

L. Ron Hubbard developed just such a method, and it is applicable to all men, without exception.

With this data, it is possible to accurately predict the behavior of a potential spouse, a business partner, employee or friend—before you commit to a relationship. The risks involved in human interaction can be avoided entirely or minimized when you can infallibly predict how people will behave.

By understanding and using the information in this booklet, all aspects of human relationships will become more productive and more fulfilling. You'll know who to associate with, who to avoid, and you will be able to help those who are mired in uncomfortable situations with others. Imagine knowing, after a very short time, how people will behave in any given circumstance. You can. Each and every time.

THE TONE SCALE

T he Tone Scale—a vital tool for any aspect of life involving one's fellows—is a scale which shows the successive emotional tones a person can experience. By "tone" is meant the momentary or continuing emotional state of a person. Emotions such as fear, anger, grief, enthusiasm and others which people experience are shown on this graduated scale.

Skillful use of this scale enables one to both predict and understand human behavior in all its manifestations.

This Tone Scale plots the descending spiral of life from full vitality and consciousness through half-vitality and half-consciousness down to death.

By various calculations about the energy of life, by observation and by test, this Tone Scale is able to give levels of behavior as life declines.

These various levels are common to all men.

When a man is nearly dead, he can be said to be in a chronic *apathy*. And he behaves in a certain way about other things. This is 0.05 on the Tone Scale.

When a man is chronically in *grief* about his losses, he is in grief. And he behaves certain ways about many things. This is 0.5 on the scale.

When a person is not yet so low as grief but realizes losses are impending, or is fixed chronically at this level by past losses, he can be said to be in *fear*. This is around 1.0 on the scale.

An individual who is fighting against threatened losses is in *anger.* And he manifests other aspects of behavior. This is 1.5.

The person who is merely suspicious that loss may take place or who has become fixed at this level is resentful. He can be said to be in *antagonism.* This is 2.0 on the scale.

Above antagonism, the situation of a person is not so good that he is enthusiastic, not so bad that he is resentful. He has lost some goals and cannot immediately locate others. He is said to be in *boredom,* or at 2.5 on the Tone Scale.

At 3.0 on the scale, a person has a *conservative,* cautious aspect toward life but is reaching his goals.

At 4.0 the individual is *enthusiastic,* happy and vital.

Very few people are natural 4.0s. A charitable average is probably around 2.8.

You have watched this scale in operation before now. Have you ever seen a child trying to acquire, let us say, a nickel? At first he is happy. He simply wants a nickel. If refused, he then explains why he wants it. If he fails to get it and did not want it badly, he becomes bored and goes away. But if he wants it badly, he will get antagonistic about it. Then he will become angry. Then, that failing, he may lie about why he wants it. That failing, he goes into grief. And if he is still refused, he finally sinks into apathy and says he doesn't want it. This is negation.

A child threatened by danger also dwindles down the scale. At first he does not appreciate that the danger is posed at him and he is quite cheerful. Then the danger, let us say it is a dog, starts to approach him. The child sees the danger but still does not believe it is for him and keeps on with his business. But his playthings "bore" him for the moment. He is a little apprehensive and not sure. Then the dog comes nearer. The child "resents him" or shows some antagonism. The dog comes nearer still. The child becomes angry and

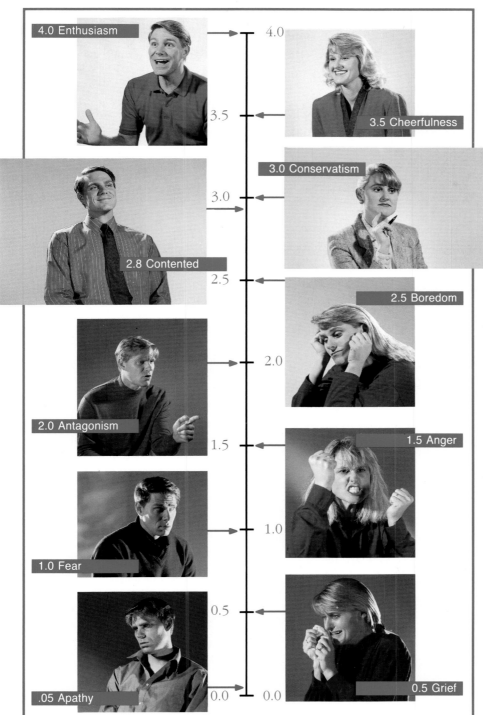

4.0 Enthusiasm

4.0

3.5 Cheerfulness

3.5

3.0 Conservatism

3.0

2.8 Contented

2.5

2.5 Boredom

2.0

2.0 Antagonism

1.5 Anger

1.5

1.0 Fear

1.0

.05 Apathy

0.5

0.5 Grief

0.0

Every person has a chronic or habitual tone. He or she moves up or down the Tone Scale as he experiences success or failure. These are temporary, or acute, tone levels. A primary goal of Scientology is to raise a person's chronic position on the Tone Scale.

makes some effort to injure the dog. The dog comes still nearer and is more threatening. The child becomes afraid. Fear unavailing, the child cries. If the dog still threatens him, the child may go into an apathy and simply wait to be bitten.

Objects or animals or people which assist survival, as they become inaccessible to the individual, bring him down the Tone Scale.

Objects, animals or people which threaten survival, as they approach the individual, bring him down the Tone Scale.

This scale has a chronic or an acute aspect. A person can be brought down the Tone Scale to a low level for ten minutes and then go back up, or he can be brought down it for ten years and not go back up.

A man who has suffered too many losses, too much pain, tends to become fixed at some lower level of the scale and, with only slight fluctuations, stays there. Then his general and common behavior will be at that level of the Tone Scale.

Just as a 0.5 moment of grief can cause a child to act along the grief band for a short while, so can a 0.5 fixation cause an individual to act 0.5 toward most things in his life.

There is momentary behavior or fixed behavior.

The Tone Scale in Full

The full Tone Scale, as can be seen on page 8, starts well below apathy. In other words, a person is feeling no emotion about a subject at all. An example of this was the American attitude concerning the atomic bomb; something about which they should have been very concerned was so far beyond their ability to control and so likely to end their existence that they were below apathy about it. They actually did not even feel that it was very much of a problem.

Feeling apathetic about the atomic bomb would be an advance over the feeling of no emotion whatsoever on a subject which should intimately concern a person. In other words, on many subjects and problems people are actually well below apathy. There the Tone Scale starts, on utter, dead null far below death itself.

Going up into improved tones one encounters the level of body death, apathy, grief, fear, anger, antagonism, boredom, enthusiasm and serenity, in that order. There are many small stops between these tones, but one knowing anything about human beings should definitely know these particular emotions. A person who is in apathy, when his tone is improved, feels grief. A person in grief, when his tone improves, feels fear. A person in fear, when his tone improves, feels anger. A person in anger, when his tone improves, feels antagonism. A person in antagonism, when his tone improves, feels boredom. When a person in boredom improves his tone, he is enthusiastic. When an enthusiastic person improves his tone, he feels serenity. Actually the below apathy level is so low as to constitute a no-affinity, no-emotion, no-problem, no-consequence state of mind on things which are actually tremendously important.

THE TONE SCALE IN FULL

40.0 Serenity of Beingness

30.0 Postulates

22.0 Games

20.0 Action

8.0 Exhilaration

6.0 Aesthetic

4.0 Enthusiasm

3.5 Cheerfulness

3.3 Strong Interest

3.0 Conservatism

2.9 Mild Interest

2.8 Contented

2.6 Disinterested

2.5 Boredom

2.4 Monotony

2.0 Antagonism

1.9 Hostility

1.8 Pain

1.5 Anger

1.4 Hate

1.3 Resentment

1.2 No Sympathy

1.15 Unexpressed Resentment

1.1 Covert Hostility

1.02 Anxiety

1.0 Fear

.98 Despair

.96 Terror

.94 Numb

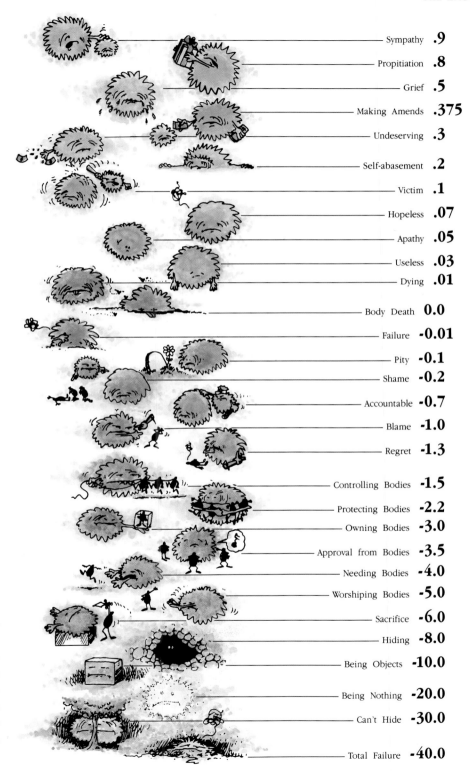

Sympathy	.9
Propitiation	.8
Grief	.5
Making Amends	.375
Undeserving	.3
Self-abasement	.2
Victim	.1
Hopeless	.07
Apathy	.05
Useless	.03
Dying	.01
Body Death	0.0
Failure	-0.01
Pity	-0.1
Shame	-0.2
Accountable	-0.7
Blame	-1.0
Regret	-1.3
Controlling Bodies	-1.5
Protecting Bodies	-2.2
Owning Bodies	-3.0
Approval from Bodies	-3.5
Needing Bodies	-4.0
Worshiping Bodies	-5.0
Sacrifice	-6.0
Hiding	-8.0
Being Objects	-10.0
Being Nothing	-20.0
Can't Hide	-30.0
Total Failure	-40.0

Characteristics on the Tone Scale

The area below apathy is an area without pain, interest, or anything else that matters to anyone, but it is an area of grave danger since one is below the level of being able to respond to anything and may accordingly lose everything without apparently noticing it.

A workman who is in very bad condition and who is actually a liability to the organization may not be capable of experiencing pain or any emotion on any subject. He is below apathy. We have seen workmen who would hurt their hand and think nothing of it and go right on working even though their hand was very badly injured. People working in medical offices and hospitals in industrial areas are quite amazed sometimes to discover how little attention some workmen pay to their own injuries. It is an ugly fact that people who pay no attention to their own injuries and who are not even feeling pain from those injuries are not and never will be, without some attention from a Scientologist, efficient people. They are liabilities to have around. They do not respond properly. If such a person is working a crane and the crane suddenly goes out of control to dump its load on a group of men, that subapathy crane operator will simply let the crane drop its load. In other words, he is a potential murderer. He cannot stop anything, he cannot change anything and he cannot start anything and yet, on some automatic response basis, he manages some of the time to hold down a job, but the moment a real emergency confronts him he is not likely to respond properly and accidents result.

Where there are accidents in industry they stem from these people in the subapathy tone range. Where bad mistakes are made in offices which cost firms a great deal of money, lost time and cause other personnel difficulties, such mistakes are found rather uniformly to stem from these subapathy people. So do not think that one of these states of being unable to feel anything, of being numb, of being incapable of pain or joy is any use to anyone. It is not. A person who is in this condition cannot control things and in actuality is not *there* sufficiently to be controlled by anyone else and does strange and unpredictable things.

Just as a person can be chronically in subapathy, so a person can be in apathy. This is dangerous enough but is at least expressed. Communication from the person himself, not from some training pattern is to be expected. People can be chronically in grief, chronically in fear, chronically in anger, or in antagonism, or boredom, or actually can be "stuck in enthusiasm." A person who is truly able is normally fairly serene about things. He can, however, express other emotions. It is a mistake to believe that a total serenity is of any real value. When a situation which demands tears cannot be cried about, one is not in serenity as a chronic tone. Serenity can be mistaken rather easily for subapathy, but of course only by a very untrained observer. One glance at the physical condition of the person is enough to differentiate. People who are in subapathy are normally quite ill.

On the level of each of the emotions we have a communication factor. In subapathy an individual is not really communicating at all. Some social response or training pattern or, as we say, "circuit" is communicating. The person himself does not seem to be there and isn't really talking. Therefore his communications are sometimes strange to say the least. He does the wrong things at the wrong time. He says the wrong things at the wrong time.

Naturally when a person is stuck on any of the bands of the Tone Scale—subapathy, apathy, grief, fear, anger, antagonism, boredom, enthusiasm or serenity—he voices communications with that emotional tone. A person who is always angry about something is stuck in anger. Such a person is not as bad off as somebody in subapathy, but he is still rather dangerous to have around since he will make trouble, and a person who is angry does not control things well. The communication characteristics of people at these various levels on the Tone Scale are quite fascinating. They say things and handle communication each in a distinct characteristic fashion for each level of the Tone Scale.

There is also a level of reality for each of the levels of the Tone Scale. Reality is an intensely interesting subject since it has to do, in the main, with relative solids. In other words, the solidity of things and the emotional tone of people have a definite connection. People low on the Tone Scale cannot tolerate solids. They cannot tolerate a solid object. The thing is not real to them; it is thin or lacking weight. As they come up scale, the same object becomes more and more solid and they can finally see it in its true level of solidity. In other words, these people have a definite reaction to mass at various points on the scale. Things are bright to them or very, very dull. If you could look through the eyes of the person in subapathy you would see a very watery, thin, dreamy, misty, unreal world indeed. If you looked through the eyes of an angry man you would see a world which was menacingly solid, where all the solids posed a brutality toward him, but they still would not be sufficiently solid or sufficiently real or visible for a person in good condition. A person in serenity can see solids as they are, as bright as they are, and can tolerate an enormous heaviness or solidity without reacting to it. In other words, as we go up the Tone Scale from the lowest to the highest, things can get more and more solid and more and more real.

Observing the Obvious

The Tone Scale is an extremely useful tool to help predict the characteristics and behavior of a person. But to do this well you must be able to recognize a person's position on the scale at a glance.

The Tone Scale is very easy to apply on a casual basis for some acute tone. "Joe was on a 1.5 kick last night." Sure, he turned red as a beet and threw a book at your head. Simple. Mary breaks into sobs, and grabs for the Kleenex, easily recognizable as grief. But how about a person's chronic tone level? This can be masked by a thin veneer of social training and responses. Such is called a social tone. It is neither chronic, nor acute, but is a reflection of the person's social education and mannerisms adopted to present himself to others. How sharp and how certain are you about that? Take a person that you are familiar with. What, exactly, is his chronic tone?

There is a word "obnosis" which has been put together from the phrase, "observing the obvious." The art of observing the obvious is strenuously neglected in our society at this time. Pity. It's the only way you ever see anything; you observe the obvious. You look at the isness of something, at what is actually there. Fortunately for us, the ability to obnose is not in any sense "inborn" or mystical. But it is being taught that way by people outside of Scientology.

How do you teach somebody to see what is there? Well, you put up something for him to look at, and have him tell you what he sees. An individual can practice this on his own or in a group situation, such as a class. One simply selects a person or object and observes what is *there*. In a classroom situation, for instance, a student is asked to stand up in the front of the room and be looked at by the rest of the students. An instructor stands by, and asks the students:

"What do you see?"

The first responses run about like this:

"Well, I can see he's had a lot of experience."

"Oh, can you? Can you really see his experience? What do you see there?"

"Well, I can tell from the wrinkles around his eyes and mouth that he's had lots of experience."

"All right, but what do you see?"

"Oh, I get you. I see wrinkles around his eyes and mouth."

"Good!"

The instructor accepts nothing that is not plainly visible.

A student starts to catch on and says, "Well, I can really see he's got ears."

"All right, but from where you're sitting can you see both ears right now as you're looking at him?"

"Well, no."

"Okay. What do you see?"

"I see he's got a left ear."

"Fine!"

No guesses, no assumptions will do. For example, "He's got good posture."

"Good posture by comparison with what?"

"Well, he's standing straighter than most people I've seen."

"Are they here now?"

"Well, no, but I've got memories of them."

"Come on. Good posture in relation to what, that you can see right now."

"Well, he's standing straighter than you are. You're a little slouched."

"Right this minute?"

"Yes."

"Very good."

The goal of such drilling is to get a student to the point where he can look at another person, or an object, and see exactly what is there. Not a deduction of what might be there from what he does see there. Just what is there, visible and plain to the eye. It's so simple, it hurts.

You can get a good tip on chronic tone from what a person does with his eyes. At apathy, he will give the appearance of looking fixedly, for minutes on end, at a particular object. The only thing is, he doesn't see it. He isn't aware of the object at all. If you dropped a bag over his head, the focus of his eyes would probably remain the same.

Moving up to grief, the person does look "downcast." A person in chronic grief tends to focus his eyes down in the direction of the floor a good bit. In the lower ranges of grief, his attention will be fairly fixed, as in apathy. As he starts moving up into the fear band, you get the focus shifting around, but still directed downward.

At fear itself, the very obvious characteristic is that the person can't look at you. People are too dangerous to look at. He's supposedly talking to you, but he's looking over in left field. Then he glances at your feet briefly, then over your head (you get the impression a

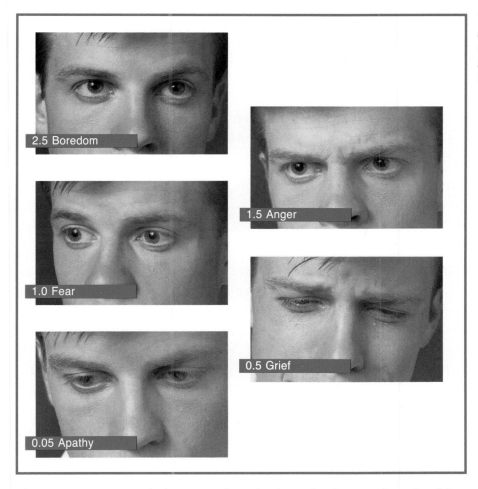

2.5 Boredom

1.5 Anger

1.0 Fear

0.5 Grief

0.05 Apathy

plane's passing over), but now he's looking back over his shoulder. Flick, flick, flick. In short, he'll look anywhere but at you.

Then, in the lower band of anger, he will look away from you, deliberately. He looks *away* from you; it's an overt communication break. A little further up the line and he'll look directly at you all right, but not very pleasantly. He wants to locate you—as a target.

Then, at boredom, you get the eyes wandering around again, but not frantically as in fear. Also, he won't be avoiding looking at you. He'll include you among the things he looks at.

Equipped with data of this sort, and having gained some proficiency in the obnosis of people, a person can next go out into the public to talk to strangers and spot them on the Tone Scale. Usually, but only as a slight crutch in approaching people, a person doing this should have a series of questions to ask each person, and a clipboard for jotting down the answers, notes, etc. The real purpose of their talking to people at all is to spot them on the Tone Scale, chronic tone and social tone. They are given questions calculated to produce lags and break through social training and education, so that the chronic tone juts out.

Here are some sample questions used for this drill: "What's the most obvious thing about me?" "When was the last time you had your hair cut?" "Do you think people do as much work now as they did fifty years ago?"

At first, the persons doing this merely spot the tone of the person they are interviewing—and many and various are the adventures they have while doing this! Later, as they gain some assurance about stopping strangers and asking them questions, these instructions are added: "Interview at least fifteen people. With the first five, match their tone, as soon as you've spotted it. The next five, you drop below their chronic tone, and see what happens. For the last five, put on a higher tone than theirs."

What can a person gain from these exercises? A willingness to communicate with anyone, for one thing. To begin with, a person can be highly selective about the sort of people he stops. Only old ladies. No one who looks angry. Or only people who look clean. Finally, they just stop the next person who comes along, even though he looks leprous and armed to the teeth. Their ability to confront people has come way up, and a person is just somebody else to talk to. They become willing to pinpoint a person on the scale, without wavering or hesitating.

They also become quite gifted and flexible at assuming tones at will, and putting them across convincingly, which is very useful in many situations, and lots of fun to do.

Being able to recognize the tone level of people at a single glance is an ability which can give a tremendous advantage in one's dealings with others. It is a skill well worth the time and effort to acquire.

THE HUBBARD CHART OF HUMAN EVALUATION

The whole subject of how to accurately judge our fellows is something that man has wanted to be able to do for a long time. In Scientology we have a chart which shows a way one can precisely evaluate human behavior and predict what a person will do.

This is the Hubbard Chart of Human Evaluation, a foldout copy of which is at the back of this booklet.

The chart displays the degree of ethics, responsibility, persistence on a given course, handling of truth and other identifying aspects of a person along the various levels of the Tone Scale.

You can examine the chart and you will find in the boxes, as you go across it, the various characteristics of people at these levels. Horribly enough these characteristics have been found to be constant. If you have a 3.0 as your rating, then you will carry across the whole chart at 3.0.

If you can locate two or three characteristics along a certain level of this scale, you can look in the number column opposite those characteristics and find the level. It may be 2.5, it may be 1.5. Wherever it is, simply look at *all* the columns opposite the number you found and you will see the remaining characteristics.

The only mistake you can make in evaluating somebody else on this Tone Scale is to assume that he departs from it somewhere and is higher in one department than he is in another. The characteristic may be masked to which you object—but it is there.

Look at the top of the first column and you get a general picture of the behavior and physiology of the person. Look at the second column for the physical condition. Look at the third column for the most generally expressed emotion of the person. Continue on across the various columns. Somewhere you will find data about somebody or yourself of which you can be sure. Then simply examine all the other boxes at the level of the data you were certain about. That band, be it 1.5 or 3.0, will tell you the story of a human being.

Of course, as good news and bad, happy days and sad ones, strike a person, there are momentary raises and lowerings on this Tone Scale. But, as mentioned, there is a chronic level, an average behavior for each individual.

As an individual is found lower and lower on this chart, so is his alertness, his consciousness lower and lower.

The individual's chronic mood or attitude toward existence declines in direct ratio to the way he regards the physical universe and organisms about him.

It is not a complete statement to say, merely, that one becomes fixed in his regard for the physical universe and organisms about him, for there are definite ways, beyond consciousness, which permit this to take place. Manifestation, however, is a decline of consciousness with regard to the physical environment of an individual. That decline of consciousness is a partial cause of a gradual sag down this chart, but it is illustrative enough for our purposes in this volume.

The position of an individual on this Tone Scale varies through the day and throughout the years but is fairly stable for given periods. One's position on the chart will rise on receipt of good news, sink with bad news. This is the usual give and take with life. Everyone however has a *chronic* position on the chart which is unalterable save for Scientology processing.

Scientology processing is a very unique form of personal counseling which helps an individual look at his own existence and improves his ability to confront what he is and where he is. Processing thus raises the chronic tone of that individual.

On the other hand, on an acute basis, necessity level (lifting oneself by one's bootstraps as in emergencies) can raise an individual well up this chart for brief periods.

One's environment also greatly influences one's position on the chart. Every environment has its own tone level. A man who is really a 3.0 can begin to act like a 1.1 (covert hostility) in a 1.1 environment. However, a 1.1 usually acts no better than about 1.5 in an environment with a high tone. If one lives in a low-toned environment he can expect, eventually, to be low-toned. This is also true of marriage—one tends to match the tone level of one's marital partner.

This Tone Scale is also valid for groups. A business or a nation can be examined as to its various standard reactions and these can be plotted. This will give the survival potential of a business or a nation.

This chart can also be used in employing people or in choosing partners. It is an accurate index of what to expect and gives you a chance to predict what people will do before you have any great experience with them. Also, it gives you some clue as to what can happen to you in certain environments or around certain people, for they can drag you down or boost you high.

However, don't use this chart as an effort to make somebody knuckle under. Don't tell people where they are on it. It may ruin them. Let them take their own examinations.

A Tone Scale Test

Probably the most accurate index of a person's position on the Tone Scale is speech.

Unless a person talks openly and listens receptively he cannot be considered very high on the Tone Scale.

In column 10 of the Hubbard Chart of Human Evaluation, "Speech: Talks/Speech: Listens," there are double boxes: one set referring to talking, the other to listening. It may not have occurred to some people that communication is both outflow and inflow. An observation of how a person both listens and talks will give an accurate indication of his position on the Tone Scale.

An individual can be lifted only about half a point on the Tone Scale by conversation.

By responding to a person's anger with boredom, a person's tone can be lifted.

It is interesting to note that with this column one can conduct what we call a "two-minute psychometry" on someone. *Psychometry* is the measurement of mental traits, abilities and processes. The way to do a two-minute psychometry is simply to start talking to the person at the highest possible tone level, creatively and constructively, and then gradually drop the tone of one's conversation down to the point where it achieves response from the person. An individual best responds to his own tone band; and an individual can be lifted only about half a point on the Tone Scale by conversation. In doing this type of "psychometry," one should not carry any particular band of conversation too long, not more than a sentence or two, because this will have a tendency to raise slightly the tone of the person and so spoil the accuracy of the test.

Two-minute psychometry, then, is done, first, by announcing something creative and constructive and seeing whether the person responds in kind; then, giving forth some casual conversation, perhaps about sports, and seeing if the person responds to that. Getting no response start talking antagonistically about things about which the person knows—but not, of course, about the person—to see if he achieves a response at this point. Then give forth with a sentence or two of anger against some condition. Then indulge in a small amount of discreditable gossip and see if there is any response to that. If this does not work, then dredge up some statements of hopelessness and misery. Somewhere in this range the person will agree with the type of conversation that is being offered—that is, he will respond to it in kind. A conversation can then be carried on along this band where the person has been discovered, and one will rapidly gain enough information to make a good first estimate of the person's position on the chart.

This two-minute psychometry by conversation can also be applied to groups. That speaker who desires to command his audience must not talk above or below his audience's tone more than half a point. If he wishes to lift the audience's tone, he should talk about half a point above their general tone level. An expert speaker, using this two-minute psychometry and carefully noting the responses of his audience, can, in two minutes, discover the tone of the audience—whereupon, all he has to do is adopt a tone slightly above theirs.

The Tone Scale and the Chart of Human Evaluation are the most important tools ever developed for the prediction of human behavior. Employ these tools and you will at all times know who you are dealing with, who to associate with, who to trust. ■

PRACTICAL EXERCISES

The following exercises will help you understand this booklet and increase your ability to actually apply the knowledge it contains.

1 Using the Hubbard Chart of Human Evaluation, consider five people you know and determine the chronic tone level for each. (Do not tell the person what you determined his tone level to be.)

2 Practice obnosis. Look around your environment and practice seeing what is there. Notice things which are plainly obvious. Don't allow any assumption into your observation. Continue to practice obnosis until you are sure you can do it without adding in any assumptions.

3 Spot the tone levels of different people. Go to a place where there are lots of people. Pick out a person and notice his or her tone level. Do this again and again with different people. Observe people in conversation or engaging in some activity and note their tone levels. Continue doing this until you are confident you can spot the tone level of people by observing them. (Do not tell the people you observe what tone level you think them to be in, however.)

4 Practice spotting the tone levels of people by engaging them in conversation. Take a clipboard and paper and interview people on the street. Ask them some sample questions such as "What's the most obvious thing about me?" "When was the last time you had a haircut?" "Do you think people do as much work now as they did fifty years ago?" Other questions of a similar nature can be used to gain responses from the person. Determine the person's tone level based on his responses. Is there a social tone sitting atop his chronic tone? Repeat the interview with other people, noting the person's tone level each time. Keep this up until you can approach anyone and engage him in conversation and determine his chronic tone level. (Important note: Do not tell the person what tone level you observe him to be in, or evaluate his tone level for him.)

5 When you have gained assurance at Exercise 4, interview more people. Interview at least fifteen people. With the first five, match their tone as soon as you have spotted it. With the next five, drop below their chronic tone and see what happens. For the last five, put on a higher tone than theirs. Note down your observations from doing this. Practice this with more people until you are confident you can spot a person's tone level and then match it, drop below it or assume a tone above it.

6 Do a two-minute psychometry on a person. Engage a person in a conversation and, using the technique given in the booklet, determine what tone level the person responds to. Repeat this with other people until you are confident you can spot what tone level a person will respond to.

7 Practice raising a person's tone level. Engage a person in conversation. Once you have determined his tone level, adopt a tone one-half to one full tone above his. Note what happens to his tone level. Repeat this with other people until you are confident you can raise a person on the Tone Scale.

RESULTS FROM APPLICATION

Knowledge of the Tone Scale and the ability to use it has given people a new freedom when dealing with others that could not otherwise exist for them. It has given them the ability to predict the behavior of others and deal with them successfully no matter whether a person be in apathy, grief, fear, anger, antagonism, boredom, cheerfulness or enthusiasm. The skill to bring another up the Tone Scale is easily achieved with this knowledge.

Many people have found that the actions, reactions and behavior of others become highly predictable when one can observe where they are on the scale. Life is less confusing or mysterious. The health, survival potential and longevity of an individual or group can also be predicted. How another will treat his property or yours becomes obvious.

People from all walks of life: artists, performers, actors, executives, foremen and teachers all swear that use of this technology puts them in the driver's seat in life. Being able to predict the behavior of others makes life a game that you can win, as shown in the following accounts.

Knowing how people in different tone levels react made all the difference to a southern California contractor. He experienced a huge increase in his general competence upon learning this data.

"I had always been driven crazy trying to be logical in dealing with people in the lower bands of the Tone Scale, especially people in antagonism. Once I knew the data on the Tone Scale, I was no longer bothered by certain customers, particularly the antagonistic ones, I had to service. Running my business became a breeze and my personal sales statistics tripled in just a few weeks. I was much more causative in dealing with people."

Dismayed when first asked to do a sales course, a woman who worked in a telecommunications company in Florida was amazed that she could do such a job successfully. She had her own considerations about salesmen and didn't want to be "one of those annoying salespeople who call you at the most inopportune time to tell you about something you have no interest in." However, she

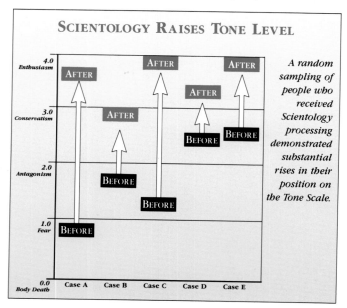

SCIENTOLOGY RAISES TONE LEVEL

A random sampling of people who received Scientology processing demonstrated substantial rises in their position on the Tone Scale.

had the good fortune to do a sales course that included data on the emotional Tone Scale.

*"I **really** enjoyed this course and the gains I got from it! I had heard about the emotional Tone Scale before, but I had no idea really how to use it. And I realized that 'bad' salesmen don't have this data, so no wonder they are annoying! Using the technology, I can now go in at the right tone level and make my sales boom!"*

In Denmark, a girl was having a problem with a friend. Something was bothering him that he would not communicate about. She tried to talk to him, but he still wouldn't say what was wrong. His reticence was creating a big upset between them. She decided to write him a very cheerful letter but, to her surprise, it had no effect on him. When she asked him about it, he told her that he couldn't even remember what it said! She eventually solved this dilemma using the Tone Scale.

"I finally realized that my communication was too high for his tone level, and thus it resulted in no communication. So I wrote him another letter which was closer to his tone level, and amazingly enough it got across to him very much! He started talking to me and we are friends again.

"If I hadn't had the technology on the Tone Scale I would have given up. This made me brave enough to write him another letter. Otherwise, I would

have gone into apathy about it and would have lost a very good friend. Instead, using the Tone Scale and communication, I brought him up the scale and salvaged our friendship!"*

A girl in Scandinavia had just broken up with her boyfriend. Although not particularly happy, she did, however, have the data on the Tone Scale. She decided to use this tool to turn around her life:

*"I had a lot of very good friends but no prospects for a boyfriend. A new guy joined our group of friends. We got in communication shortly after he joined the group and I realized that we had almost identical communication levels. He seemed like a very nice guy. I would mention that something needed to get handled and I would turn around and he would be busy handling it. He would say that we needed rolls for dinner and I was already on my way to the bakery. I would mention something and he would let me know that he just thought of this. We matched perfectly on the Tone Scale. I looked at this and was laughing to myself, as he was in no way the type of guy I would earlier have looked for. Priorly, I had always looked at appearance only which led to a hit-and-miss experience. This guy, however, was a **real** match and within weeks we decided to get married and we did."*

A young man on the East Coast found himself unable to deal with some of those he came into contact with when he moved to New York City. After a lot of trial and error he finally found the solution with the technology of the Tone Scale.

"When I first moved to the city and got a job, I found myself in a dangerous and unfriendly situation. Though the job was interesting and paid well, the unfriendliness seemed so bad that after only a few months I was seriously considering leaving the job.

"Then I attended a lecture at the Church of Scientology and learned about L. Ron Hubbard's technology on the Tone Scale. From this I realized that what I was experiencing was that a few of the people I was dealing with were at antagonism on the Tone Scale. And not only this, I was approaching them in the tone level of fear—which simply made things worse!

"From that point on, I was able to comfortably deal with others around me and I no longer took things so personally when confronted by someone in the lower tone levels. What a relief!"

A young Alaskan man used the technology of the Tone Scale to help an individual and improve the productivity of a whole group.

"Working with a group of a dozen people on a construction project, I noticed that one of my co-workers was moving slowly, making mistakes and actually slowing down the whole project. I had recently studied Mr. Hubbard's information on the Tone Scale and decided I should put it to work.

"First I observed the person and talked with him a bit, to spot where he was on the Tone Scale. Once I had done this, I started to talk to him and give him directions in a tone level a bit above his. Just as it said in the book I'd studied, his tone rose. He brightened up a bit and started working faster and taking care about what he was doing. In fact, the whole group seemed to pick up speed, just from seeing this fellow doing better!

"It felt great to be able to change a situation for the better, with such a simple action."

Familiarity with the Tone Scale helped a young Australian girl deal with a person who no one else was able to manage. She was standing in line to purchase something at a store when a ruffian began kicking things and being very rude and antagonistic.

"Nobody was controlling this man; they were just getting upset at his actions but didn't really know what to do about it. I used the Tone Scale to be at cause over the situation and just acknowledged the man using the correct level of the Tone Scale. He ended his 'performance' at once!

"The man who was standing next to me in line was amazed and said, 'I don't know what you did, but whatever it was, it handled him!' "

GLOSSARY

affinity: love, liking or any other emotional attitude; the degree of liking. The basic definition of affinity is the consideration of distance, whether good or bad.

beingness: condition or state of being; existence. *Beingness* also refers to the assumption or choosing of a category of identity. Beingness can be assumed by oneself or given to oneself or attained. Examples of beingness would be one's own name, one's profession, one's physical characteristics, one's role in a game—each or all of these could be called one's beingness.

case: a general term for a person being treated or helped.

comm: short for *communication. See also* **communication** in this glossary.

communication: an interchange of ideas across space between two individuals.

confront: to face without flinching or avoiding. The ability to confront is actually the ability to be there comfortably and perceive.

entheta: enturbulated theta; especially referring to communications, which, based on lies and confusions, are slanderous, choppy or destructive in an attempt to overwhelm or suppress a person or group. *See also* **enturbulate** and **theta** in this glossary.

enturbulate: put into a state of agitation or disturbance.

ethics: the actions an individual takes on himself to correct some conduct or situation in which he is involved which is contrary to the ideals and best interests of his group. It is a personal thing. When one is ethical or "has his ethics in," it is by his own determinism and is done by himself.

Hubbard Chart of Human Evaluation: a chart by which one can precisely evaluate human behavior and predict what a person will do. It displays the various characteristics that exist at different levels of the Tone Scale.

invalidate: refute, degrade, discredit or deny something someone else considers to be fact.

mass: the actual physical objects, the things of life.

obnosis: a coined word put together from "observing the obvious." It is the action of a person looking at another person or an object and seeing exactly what is there, not a deduction of what might be there from what he does see.

postulate: a conclusion, decision or resolution about something.

present time: the time which is now and becomes the past as rapidly as it is observed. It is a term loosely applied to the environment existing in now.

process: an exact series of directions or sequence of actions taken to accomplish a desired result.

processing: a special form of personal counseling, unique in Scientology, which helps an individual look at his own existence and improves his ability to confront what he is and where he is. It thus raises the chronic tone of that individual. Processing is a precise, thoroughly codified activity with exact procedures.

reality: that which appears to be. Reality is fundamentally agreement; the degree of agreement reached by people. What we agree to be real is real.

Scientology: an applied religious philosophy developed by L. Ron Hubbard. It is the study and handling of the spirit in relationship to itself, universes and other life. The word *Scientology* comes from the Latin *scio*, which means "know" and the Greek word *logos*, meaning "the word or outward form by which the inward thought is expressed and made known." Thus, Scientology means knowing about knowing.

theta: thought or life. The term comes from the Greek letter *theta (θ)*, which the Greeks used to represent *thought* or perhaps *spirit.* Something which is *theta* is characterized by reason, serenity, stability, happiness, cheerful emotion, persistence and the other factors which man ordinarily considers desirable.

Tone Scale: a scale which shows the successive emotional tones a person can experience. By "tone" is meant the momentary or continuing emotional state of a person. Emotions such as fear, anger, grief, enthusiasm and others which people experience are shown on this graduated scale.

About L. Ron Hubbard

No more fitting statement typifies the life of L. Ron Hubbard than his simple declaration: "I like to help others and count it as my greatest pleasure in life to see a person free himself from the shadows which darken his days." Behind these pivotal words stands a lifetime of service to mankind and a legacy of wisdom that enables anyone to attain long-cherished dreams of happiness and spiritual freedom.

Born in Tilden, Nebraska on March 13, 1911, his road of discovery and dedication to his fellows began at an early age. "I wanted other people to be happy, and could not understand why they weren't," he wrote of his youth; and therein lay the sentiments that would long guide his steps. By the age of nineteen, he had traveled more than a quarter of a million miles, examining the cultures of Java, Japan, India and the Philippines.

Returning to the United States in 1929, Ron resumed his formal education and studied mathematics, engineering and the then new field of nuclear physics—all providing vital tools for continued research. To finance that research, Ron embarked upon a literary career in the early 1930s, and soon became one of the most widely read authors of popular fiction. Yet never losing sight of his primary goal, he continued his mainline research through extensive travel and expeditions.

With the advent of World War II, he entered the United States Navy as a lieutenant (junior grade) and served as commander of antisubmarine corvettes. Left partially blind and lame from injuries sustained during combat, he was diagnosed as permanently disabled by 1945. Through application of his theories on the mind, however, he was not only able to help fellow servicemen, but also to regain his own health.

After five more years of intensive research, Ron's discoveries were presented to the world in *Dianetics: The Modern Science of Mental Health.* The first popular handbook on the human mind expressly written for the man in the street, *Dianetics* ushered in a new era of hope for mankind and a new phase of life for its author. He did, however, not cease his research, and as breakthrough after breakthrough was carefully codified through late 1951, the applied religious philosophy of Scientology was born.

Because Scientology explains the whole of life, there is no aspect of man's existence that L. Ron Hubbard's subsequent work did not address. Residing variously in the United States and England, his continued research brought forth solutions to such social ills as declining educational standards and pandemic drug abuse.

All told, L. Ron Hubbard's works on Scientology and Dianetics total forty million words of recorded lectures, books and writings. Together, these constitute the legacy of a lifetime that ended on January 24, 1986. Yet the passing of L. Ron Hubbard in no way constituted an end; for with a hundred million of his books in circulation and millions of people daily applying his technologies for betterment, it can truly be said the world still has no greater friend. ■

CHURCHES OF SCIENTOLOGY

WESTERN UNITED STATES

Church of Scientology of Arizona
2111 W. University Dr.
Mesa, Arizona 85201

Church of Scientology of the Valley
3619 West Magnolia Boulevard
Burbank, California 91506

Church of Scientology of Los Angeles
4810 Sunset Boulevard
Los Angeles, California 90027

Church of Scientology of Mountain View
2483 Old Middlefield Way
Mountain View, California 96043

Church of Scientology of Pasadena
263 E. Colorado Boulevard
Pasadena, California 91101

Church of Scientology of Sacramento
825 15th Street
Sacramento, California 95814

Church of Scientology of San Diego
635 "C" Street, Suite 200
San Diego, California 92101

Church of Scientology of San Francisco
83 McAllister Street
San Francisco, California 94102

Church of Scientology of Stevens Creek
80 E. Rosemary
San Jose, California 95112

Church of Scientology of Santa Barbara
524 State Street
Santa Barbara, California 93101

Church of Scientology of Orange County
1451 Irvine Boulevard
Tustin, California 92680

Church of Scientology of Colorado
375 S. Navajo Street
Denver, Colorado 80223

Church of Scientology of Hawaii
1146 Bethel Street
Honolulu, Hawaii 96813

Church of Scientology of Minnesota
Twin Cities
1011 Nicollet Mall
Minneapolis, Minnesota 55403

Church of Scientology of Kansas City
3619 Broadway
Kansas City, Missouri 64111

Church of Scientology of Missouri
9510 Page Boulevard
St. Louis, Missouri 63132

Church of Scientology of Nevada
846 E. Sahara Avenue
Las Vegas, Nevada 89104

Church of Scientology of New Mexico
8106 Menaul Boulevard N.E.
Albuquerque, New Mexico 87110

Church of Scientology of Portland
323 S.W. Washington
Portland, Oregon 97204

Church of Scientology of Texas
2200 Guadalupe
Austin, Texas 78705

Church of Scientology of Utah
1931 S. 1100 East
Salt Lake City, Utah 84106

Church of Scientology of Washington State
2226 3rd Avenue
Seattle, Washington 98121

EASTERN UNITED STATES

Church of Scientology of Connecticut
909 Whalley Avenue
New Haven, Connecticut 06515

Church of Scientology of Florida
120 Giralda Avenue
Coral Gables, Florida 33134

Church of Scientology of Orlando
1830 East Colonial Drive
Orlando, Florida 32803

Church of Scientology of Tampa
3617 Henderson Boulevard
Tampa, Florida 33609

Church of Scientology of Georgia
2632 Piedmont Road, N.E.
Atlanta, Georgia 30324

Church of Scientology of Illinois
3011 N. Lincoln Avenue
Chicago, Illinois 60657

Church of Scientology of Boston
448 Beacon Street
Boston, Massachusetts 02115

Church of Scientology of Ann Arbor
2355 West Stadium Boulevard
Ann Arbor, Michigan 48103

Church of Scientology of Michigan
321 Williams Street
Royal Oak, Michigan 48067

Church of Scientology of Buffalo
47 West Huron Street
Buffalo, New York 14202

Church of Scientology of Long Island
99 Railroad Station Plaza
Hicksville, New York 11801

Church of Scientology of New York
227 West 46th Street
New York City, New York 10036

Church of Scientology of Cincinnati
215 West 4th Street, 5th Floor
Cincinnati, Ohio 45202

Church of Scientology of Ohio
30 North High Street
Columbus, Ohio 43215

Church of Scientology of Pennsylvania
1315 Race Street
Philadelphia, Pennsylvania 19107

Founding Church of Scientology of Washington, DC
2125 "S" Street N.W.
Washington, DC 20008

PUERTO RICO

Church of Scientology of Puerto Rico
272 JT Piniero Avenue
Hyde Park, Hato Rey
Puerto Rico 00918

UNITED KINGDOM

Church of Scientology of Birmingham
Albert House, 3rd Floor
24 Albert Street
Birmingham
England B4 7UD

Church of Scientology of Brighton
5 St. Georges Place
London Road
Brighton, Sussex
England BN1 4GA

Church of Scientology Saint Hill Foundation
Saint Hill Manor
East Grinstead, West Sussex
England RH19 4JY

Church of Scientology of London
68 Tottenham Court Road
London
England W1P 0BB

Church of Scientology of Manchester
258 Deansgate
Manchester
England M3 4BG

Church of Scientology of Plymouth
41 Ebrington Street
Plymouth, Devon
England PL4 9AA

Church of Scientology of Sunderland
51 Fawcett Street
Sunderland, Tyne and Wear
England SR1 1RS

Hubbard Academy of Personal Independence
20 Southbridge
Edinburgh
Scotland EH1 1LL

EUROPE

Austria

Church of Scientology of Austria
Schottenfeldgasse 13/15
1070 Wien

Belgium

Church of Scientology of Belgium
61, rue du Prince Royal
1050 Bruxelles

Denmark

Church of Scientology of Jylland
Guldsmedegade 17, 2
8000 Aarhus C

Church of Scientology of Copenhagen
Store Kongensgade 55
1264 Copenhagen K

Church of Scientology of Denmark
Gammel Kongevej 3–5, 1
1610 Copenhagen V

France

Church of Scientology of Angers
10–12, rue Max Richard
49100 Angers

Church of Scientology of Clermont-Ferrand
1, rue Ballainvilliers
63000 Clermont-Ferrand

Church of Scientology of Lyon
3, place des Capucins
69001 Lyon

Church of Scientology of Paris
65, rue de Dunkerque
75009 Paris

Church of Scientology of Saint-Étienne
24, rue Marengo
42000 Saint-Étienne

Germany

Church of Scientology of Berlin
Sponholzstraße 51–52
12159 Berlin

Church of Scientology of Düsseldorf
Friedrichstraße 28
40217 Düsseldorf

Church of Scientology of Frankfurt
Darmstädter Landstraße 213
60598 Frankfurt

Church of Scientology of Hamburg
Steindamm 63
20099 Hamburg

Church of Scientology of Hanover
Hubertusstraße 2
30163 Hannover

Church of Scientology of Munich
Beichstraße 12
80802 München

Church of Scientology of Stuttgart
Urbanstraße 70
70182 Stuttgart

Israel

Dianetics and Scientology College of Israel
42 Gorden Street, 2nd Floor
Tel Aviv 66023

Italy

Church of Scientology of Brescia
Via Fratelli Bronzetti, 20
25125 Brescia

Church of Scientology of Catania
Via Garibaldi, 9
95121 Catania

Church of Scientology of Milan
Via Abetone, 10
20137 Milano

Church of Scientology of Monza
Via Cavour, 5
20052 Monza

Church of Scientology of Novara
Corso Cavallotti, 7
28100 Novara

Church of Scientology of Nuoro
Via Lamarmora, 115
08100 Nuoro

Church of Scientology of Padua
Via Mameli, 1/5
35131 Padova